GILLIAN
ALLNUTT

Beginning the Avocado

VIRAGO

First published by VIRAGO PRESS Limited 1987
41 William IV Street, London WC2N 4DB

British Library Cataloguing in Publication Data
Allnutt, Gillian
Beginning the avocado.
I. Title
821′.914 PR6051.L545/

ISBN 0-86068-832-1

Photoset by Rowland Phototypesetting Limited,
Bury St Edmunds, Suffolk
Printed in Great Britain by
Anchor Brendon, Tiptree, Essex

'Lizzie Siddall: Her Journal [1862]' was published as a pamphlet by The Greville Press in 1985. 'Why Not' won first prize in the Stroud Festival International Poetry Competition in 1978. Some of the poems have previously appeared in the following anthologies and magazines: *Ambit*; *Angels of Fire: An Anthology of Radical Poetry in the '80s*; *Eve Before the Holocaust*; *The Literary Review*; *New Poetry 6*; *Schreiben* (West Germany); *Sea-Legs*; *The Sister Seven Poster Exhibition*; *Sow's Ear*; *Spinster*; *The Third Eye*; *Writing Women*.

For John Levinson
(1949–1979)

Contents

Ode

'To depict a (bicycle), you must first come to love (it).' Alexander Blok

I swear by every rule in the bicycle
owner's manual

that I love you, I, who have repeatedly,
painstakingly,

with accompanying declaration of despair,
tried to repair

you, to patch things up,
to maintain a workable relationship.

I have spent sleepless nights
in pondering your parts – those private

and those that all who walk the street
may look at –

wondering what makes you tick
over smoothly, or squeak.

O my trusty steed,
my rusty three-speed,

I would feed you the best oats
if oats

were applicable.
Only linseed oil

will do
to nourish you.

I want
so much to paint

you,
midnight blue

mudgutter black
and standing as you do, ironic

at the rail
provided by the Council –

beautiful
the sun caught in your back wheel –

or at home in the hall, remarkable
among other bicycles,

your handlebars erect.
Allow me to depict

you thus. And though I can't do justice
to your true opinion of the surface

of the road –
put into words

the nice distinctions that you make
among the different sorts of tarmac –

still I'd like to set the record of our travels straight.
I'd have you know that

not with three-in-one
but with my own

heart's
spittle I anoint your moving parts.

Riding Home

New Year's Eve, 1982–3

Halfway home. A school yard.
Here the learning year begins and ends.

Here stands
an Indian bean tree, like a god

whose thousand hands
are in momentous conversation with the wind.

Listen. The long pods rattle
like words

in a foreign tongue,
like worry beads.

The wind is all
fingers and thumbs.

The wheels of my bicycle and the stars
turn still.

Many hands
make light work of dreams,

but mine, being dumb, need
cards to understand,

to make a poem
for a mind that can no longer think in words.

Somewhere among the cards, tonight, are symbols
for a woman and a bicycle.

Ride home, say the pods,
my strange familiars.

Show a light
to port and starboard, but

ride home by the light
of stars.

My hands, afraid of the singing
in them, but afraid of being

still, tonight spill white wine
on a fine old carpet

in somebody else's
house

before they will come
home.

In the poem is a school yard, empty.
Only a tree stands there.

In the poem my hands are holding a star
they have rescued.

It is the white flower
of the catalpa.

It is a word
in my ear,

for I am still
in the habit of prayer.

As long ago as stars, my hands
learned how to do it,

as I learned to ride a bicycle
and can't forget.

convent

a fistful of notes
my heart

a thin must
covers the keyboard of ivory soldiers

girls are expected
to wear gloves

and a labour of love is lost
in plain sewing

each finger stitched
to the palm

the loose hem of the street
catches me

the tune
of a barrel organ

the monkey
playing alone

streetheart
no penny can buy it

I ought
to give my pocket

money for a poor child
going begging in the east

in the name of the father the son
and the monkey goes on

like the ghost
of a tell tale tit your heart shall be split

while the bell rings for angelus
here are gloves of silk a purse

on a string
worn over the shoulder

and nothing
in it

after prayers
there will be bread and butter soldiers

a measure of milk
plainsong

Two Sketches

for Monica and Alice

1 **Hiroshima, 1945**

Kasa promises. She walks
carefully all the way back
from the shop.

She has one foot on the step
when the sun slips. Her shadow stops.
She looks up.

The sun
does not fall down
until late in the afternoon.

That is a promise. It has been
given to us.
It is only eight fifteen.

She is bringing a bottle of rice wine.
It is precious.
There will be a celebration.

The house is gone.
Kasa stops. There is a shadow on the step
looking up.

2 Birmingham, 1983

Alice examines the shadow
that lies before her
like a future.

It is fantastic:
an elegant woman dressed in black,
an old one bent over a stick.

Alice stops short.
She is only eight,
but she can just imagine it.

Alice, come on up.
The sun has reached the bottom of the step.
It is quarter past eight.

Tomorrow is
another day. That is a promise.
Come.

Alice forgets her shadow. Carelessly
it hops before her
two steps at a time.

At Dinner

Sophia, I have not forgiven anyone.
I called them my friends who, over dinner, called
for talk of the trouble in South Africa.

Airy and thin as bone china
was their conversation, their political acumen quick
as knives and forks of stainless steel.

Women of damask, Cambridge men, there is blood on my hands.
They were kind to you, my friend.
They asked no questions.

Sophia, what were you pondering in your heart?
You smiled that night, I remember,
and folded your napkin with care.

Sophia, called in her own country, South Africa, a Coloured woman, was a friend for the four years she lived in this country in the mid-1970s.

Bright Cambridge Day

Here in the morning
houses look straight to the instructive eye of the sun.
Windows are uncracked, ready for new light.
Only the sideways are dark with compressed night and the
  unconsidered moon.
Walls stand erect in the wind
that comes clean from Siberia – there being
no mountains to stop it getting here,
no lurch in the land.
It is keen, to the point.

Here the sun is unwilling
to show much heat, just enough for Good morning,
how are you? I am sober, discreet
and quite well, thank you –
when I am not. But here
I know I have to forget the dark impulsive thought
nosing up anywhere.
Here shadows are cut back
and beds made for young men before breakfast.

There are no cracks in the preserve of these English streets
and lawns so impeccable no one dares moon there
save a particular duck-billed élite
who quack only when they know how to prove
inductively or deductively
their ineluctable right to do so.
Notices neatly forbid the intruder to move.

I have come here
with a handful of sleepless nights
not to disprove anything but to know that
if I say nothing it does not exist –
I mean love that pushes up like the grass in the night,
I mean the moon in heat.
Here I can put the rind and pips of passion
in a footnote.

The sun is quiet and diligent in the many windowed court,
sedulously snipping shadows from the cloisters
until dinner time.
I see them coming then, unclamouring,
dust white hands adjusting this and that
and gowns smoothed down
down upon a multitude of unfelt meanings.

They will not howl for the rudiments of love
under a still born moon, still unconceptualised.
They sleep unflinching.

The growth of grasses stalls in the exacting wind.

Metaphysical

You alone are – what
there is: the water, me, a series
of reflections, discontinuous –

Like you to get in and out
of boats, so – unexpectedly.

Tilting the sky at will –
you hand me your soul
as if it were a punt pole
I must learn to get along with,
awkwardly.

I am impaled.
The river's made a fool of me.

Where in the world is now?

Is it what you drown in, or where I –
pole slowly on?

after a year the cherry blossom is here again

for John

I remember ironing my dress

the formal statement
                                        Bach sonata drawn
from one violin in the quiet meetinghouse
brightness caught in a high window

they laid you under the grass   I remember
the formal emotion   our bone stiff standing   thinking
are we old enough to know this
where is sadness

I for hours holding a battered cigarette
in a cold hand   match after match going out
in a scattering wind
                                        the cherry flowers mad with it

autumnal

mother of chamomile
light and the late pale flower
of november

do you remember
the pebbled bed
of the pool

and the tea cloud
boat   sailing
over the hill

Agoraphobia

The morning lies
at anchor and the house-
work ties it to me
like an ark.

But my heart is
still in its nightdress.
It potters
aimlessly

takes off its housecoat but cannot
shake off the smell
of honeysuckle
that hovers. It

holds onto that,
knows very well
whatever I tell it
the morning is afloat

on wide open waters
that wash up against the wall
of the house it has
never been to yet

knows so well. It forgets
its elevenses. Hard
by the honeysuckle wall it has
the morning moored.

It is Housewives' Choice
not a lullaby
that helps me tidy my face,
get ready

just as my mother does.
But my heart refuses
to lace up its shoes.
It grieves and cannot

cut its losses, cannot
leave the honeysuckle
morning to its own
devices.

The Hangman's Beautiful Daughter

The hangman's beautiful daughter
beckons. I have never seen her

eyes that look upon
the dark side of the moon.

Stones stand in for them.
Her tongue is a guillotine.

Her hands: black glove,
black glove. She has no other name.

Since I must go alone with her,
I name her: love.

The hangman's beautiful daughter
lets down her hair.

She does not remember
I have been talking all day with her.

I have shadowed
her words

with my own
dim apprehensions,

for my hands that sought her
were

unable to pray.
Quietly

she has caught them up in the web of her
beautiful hair.

It is like water. Everywhere
drowns.

The hangman's beautiful daughter
turns.

Her eyes are a thousand and one
murders: done, done, cleanly.

Her tongue cuts short
prevarication.

She is a queen:
the moon comes to her in its coracle.

She is a practical woman:
she has bared her hands

to haul me in.

My mother the sea gives me

Alone inland where water wells
from a little mouth in the earth
a woman is beating her head on a stone.

None of the tales my mother handed down
to me hold her
heart's mountain.

She is a woman without an apron. Her truth
is forgotten. Over and over
she drowns again in my bone-river.

Postwar

for my mother

Kate, the dead lie in the longboat,
your heart. They set out
only

in your name. You would not
marry in a hurry –
though each one came

in uniform, his brief
proposal like a sail, a pocket
handkerchief, a single

letter home. The dead lie, hopeful still
beneath tarpaulin in your life
boat heart.

I do not remember them
but the light and bitter roll call
of sails

that set out: the letters of
their names spelt right
along a sea wall.

Alien

'. . . as a woman I have no country.' Virginia Woolf

I have never returned
wounded, to the white cliffs
of Dover, knowing I rule –
though a bit of shrapnel
is my heart –
over and over singing
Elizabeth and England
in the bottom of
a gunboat.

No. I walk these streets
already beautifully paved
with bones of enemies
and women. I am subject
to a proud succession,
brave and noble sons
in mufti, bowler hats.

Who point to our great poets
with their walking sticks
of oak. Who will not bury
my heart in Westminster Abbey,
singing God the Father God
the Son and God the Holy Ghost,
this morning the serving maid
burned the toast.

Eliza sits below stairs to mend
the linen here in England's
green and pleasant –

and this land is my land
to which I have never returned.

Comfortable Words

for Irina Ratushinskaya

Slowly the sugar dissolves in the tall glass of tea.
It is a hard oblong.

You can let go of your name, now, like a silver spoon
that looked after you. Little by little love will look out of you

as Kiev looks out of its windows at the unbelievable.
Three winters of barbed wire.

Try not to remember, try not to forget: you have inherited
the earth, your samovar.

For you it is obdurate as truth or Russia,
tongue-tied mother.

For you it is silver quiet.
Remote

Mordovia: slowly your heart will discover how to dissolve its oblong.

In March 1983 the Russian poet Irina Ratushinskaya was sentenced to seven years' hard labour and five years' internal exile, accused of anti-Soviet agitation and propaganda. Her crime was writing poetry. She suffered beatings, force-feeding and solitary confinement in a 'strict regime' women's labour camp in the Mordovian Autonomous Republic. In October 1986 she was unexpectedly released.

In Snowdonia

And in the Forest of Beddgelert
I have been slowly
and the breath of morning there was green and quiet
was my valley
with the trustful voices of rain
and I was not in my thoughts alone.

But upon Glyder Fawr, that grey volcanic
stone upstanding, I have striven
only to speak
companionably to the mountain
and there was not one among all the wind who could
from cairn to cairn carry my word.

Epiphany (Yorkshire Dales)

for John

Solitude   your death   a drover's
road   two dry stone walls   the borders
of the earth   each stone a hand's width and the berth of God

Where blackthorn lays the wind bare to the bone
you herded stars

Why Not

for Virginia Woolf, Sylvia Plath, Marina Tsvetayeva

Still, I wait.
I cannot say it is love stops short
of the rope
or the river
the quiet caress of gas in an uncaring winter.
What then?

For I have stood by the indifferent river, choosing
the plunge
or the same walk home through the lengthening valley,
unstrengthened, holding a stone sagged
with the damp weight of the year
and fear articulating my heart
words held toneless in the teeth of the air.

And yes, taking charred cakes from the oven
intended for tea – I have tried
to see my head on the slatted shelf,
my old raw self gone in a whiff of gas
through a crack in the kitchen door,
my words in a clattered heap on the cold floor
like broken cups –
not hearing the children want more.

I still hold to the rope
that could silence the last obstinate scratch in the air.
A catch in the throat –
if I knew how,
I could quicken the quiet creak of despair
no more.

It is dark here
but it's only a crack in the pavement.
As yet words find their own way out
and I sit tight, striking matches.
Perhaps I shall go on like a cigarette
watching my ashes grow
and my small tongue of fire slow, tire.

I draw on life and wait
for the abrupt stubbing out.

the house of the dead

for John

your death left the door of the world wide open

stars began to come in   like lepers
home again

deadbody peppercorns   already dust
they are the burnt out images of love
you left behind   exhausted

there *is* a way out of this house   you said

but they brought your body to its shrivelled home

and I must call in the cold stars
warm them

wake

and she   like a tired disciple   sleeps
her head on a stone   beyond
gethsemane

god will always be
hard to talk to

love was a tree
where the wind exploded
into words

I was
shaken   my body was speaking
in tongues

I have forgotten

I kneel now among
stones that will never be
given a name

the sky   in silence   exposes
itself to me

its loneliness

it is deaf and dumb

and she   without
a word for any of this
sleeps on

Mary at Golgotha

No one can mend this
hill where the wind knows
no boundaries. The skull is
with God, the soul's thread
broken. Here

and there a star recalls
birth, a child falls somewhere
close to the earth, the mild grass
stitches up small holes and tatters
carefully.

With rags and bones a man
repairs the scattered
self, forgets this place
and sleeps.

For me, the moon's face, scarred
with resurrection, knows
there is no simple
sewing up: my own scars opening
and opening like eyes, devour
forgetfulness.

Lizzie Siddall: Her Journal [1862]

for John

Introduction

Elizabeth Eleanor Siddall (1829–1862) was the daughter of an ironmonger who later kept a shop in the Old Kent Road in London. At first apprenticed to a milliner, she was then taken up as a model by the young Pre-Raphaelite painters, posing for many of their pictures at the standard rate of a shilling an hour. She was the model for Rossetti's 'Beata Beatrix', and for the drowned 'Ophelia' – for which painting she floated fully-clothed in a bath, becoming ill as a result.

She was not 'beautiful' by Victorian standards: she had straight red hair and a plain round face with pointed features, hooded eyes and a long upper lip. Rossetti, and the other painters, 'recreated' her as a Pre-Raphaelite Woman: she lamented, 'No one cares about my soul'.

She expressed a desire to draw and thereby aroused Rossetti's interest. Eventually he married her. (On the marriage certificate her father's occupation was put down as 'optician'.) But the marriage was short-lived: Lizzie Siddall was not healthy, became addicted to laudanum and died of an overdose. With his wife, Rossetti buried his poems to her: seven years later he had her exhumed in order to retrieve the poems. It was said that her red hair was still bright.

I

Pre-Raphaelite, they say: I sit for hours
and peer at painted women in a book,
peer as into mirrors
lest my face forsake

me, and the fable of my hair,
and I not fit
the cap I often wear
so ill in his peculiarly silent heart.

2

I said to him today, I'd love to draw –
no, not another angel
but the likeness of my own poor
soul.

I think it like the moon,
a plain round saucer
or the bottom of a shallow pan.
I am the daughter of an ironmonger.

When he married me
he made the man
behind the counter write out carefully
'optician'

and he spelled it slowly for him.
I remember the morning my father died.
They said I made a prim –
a proper bride.

They had already paid me
a shilling an hour
to be
who was it now – Ophelia. Ophelia

died
by her own fair hand
they said. They made
believe she drowned

as I did in that bath
they brought me to day after day: I
held my breath
so long, I thought I would die

too. I was afraid
when they spoke of the beautiful
dead
woman in the book. They thought of her soul,

not mine,
dragged under by my own hair and the dress
I put on
every day. For better, for worse

I dared
this afternoon
to say to him in one of his indifferent moods
that I should like to be alone

awhile –
'as lonely as the moon is' – wistful phrases
please him. I said nothing of my soul,
of course.

3

'Copperknob'
my father always said,
giving the kettle a good hard rub
and 'Go to bed

now, Lizzie, or you'll lose
the lovely red
of your hair. No man will choose
you, though you thread

the finest needle
between here and Mayfair.
Look after it, girl.'
I was rare

enough to him, a sight
for sore eyes used
to the long dim days in the shop, and bright
as a kettle in the dust

behind the counter
where I played.
These days rarer, father – all those pictures –
and I think perhaps I should have stayed

at home where I belonged.
Here is a housemaid and her
row of warming pans. I may not lend
a hand to anyone. I live here with my red hair,

buried
far beneath it. It betrays
me to him. But inside
me, something tries

to live,
as if it were my own child turning
in her grave
and still, my wild red hair will go on keening,

shining
for him. Father, call me
home on kettle cleaning
day.

4

'Come to bed
now, Lizzie, do'
he pleads –
but I am slow

with buttons, slow to braid
my hair.
It is hard
to leave the mirror

alone. I do not know who I am
without her
whose loveliness is everything to him.
I am spare

in soul. I leave
my body
beautiful to him who makes believe
he beds a lady.

Beatrice may be
the one
who can undo her body
like a button,

who can let him
in
to his dream.
Unknowing and unknown,

I am beyond
the pale
and lovely land
of lady. Wakeful

now, I wait
for morning light, the bright mane of her hair
to burn out
of the mirror.

5

In bare grey light he slept
like a saint.
I crept
into his empty room – and that paint

woman was grinning as if she had risen
from the grave –
as if she had removed the stone
of love

that laid her
tenderly in earth,
that stayed her
hand, her mouth –

as if she, grinning, had grown
out of him,
had gripped the bone
of Adam

in her teeth
and stripped it of its dream,
as if at last she'd torn the truth
from him

and laughed at his little
death, alone,
and laid her lovely head upon the pale
grey stone.

She beckoned me to come
plain as I was in my nightdress,
and gave me her own name,
Beatrice.

Late this afternoon I stole
into the room
again – but she, subdued and sorrowful,
looked only out from the little window of his dream.

6

Laudanum
is half
a honeymoon – and by my little window blows laburnum,
morning brief

euphoria, the hour of butter
milk. But then the windblown
waterlight withdraws. The long dour
afternoon

grows over me, a hood, a close brown pod
and I –
my soul, my sun, my seed –
am poisoned inly.

7

She has been his
bedded
Beatrice.
He'll have his dead

soul soon enough.
Dante Gabriel's
wife
is far from well,

a walking shadow. Shorn of his wild
desire,
she fades as do the lilies of the field.
Only her hair is still on fire.

8

I, Lizzie, once a girl
growing up in the Old Kent Road,
give my soul
to God

the ironmonger.
Send word
to my father
when I am dead.

Until you let it be

Until you let it be
a member of the wedding or the wild sea's
harbour

you will need your heart,
your dowry. You will be
afraid to die.

Arran, Summer 1981

I cast
what I have been,
to walk alone among
stars, sea asters.

All my life I
have collected
stones or words
to weight the light

sheaf of papers
I call
body and soul,
herring gull.

Today wind tears
through the history
of the island I
hold in my hand.

Already
the sea has drowned
in a thousand shells
and bottles,

London is a ship
of fools that scuttle
back and forth across
a little stretch of water,

ears agog with radios,
here is
the six o'clock news.
It is just that

light sits still
among the asters
or suddenly startles
the stag on the morning hill.

And I have dwelt among the houses of the living

And I have dwelt among the houses of the living
dead, in London

where my father is a free man and my mother calls upon God
to let her in.

Only that long held loneliness, my heart
remembers them.

The hills, Northumberland, have no beginning and no end.

Who shall commend me to them?

evening in the garden

a low wind in the nettles
and behind the apple leaves
light ending

Being True

for John

You have returned yourself to bone
my shadow. Self

protective of me, still, to say –

when often, then,
I turned myself away
from you –

I loved you. My embattled shadow
burns.

I shall not spare
myself the loss
of you.

I bless you and the long bare road
begins.

am I

to go alone into the dark
interior   impenetrable home
of root and shard and stone   I am
afraid to come into my own
dour garden of desire   no dream
dispels me   here   it is my own heart
I explore   the loss of that
penultimate   my name

for laura two weeks old

our children are borrowed
the old woman said
she had never heard of god

as if you had already
dwelt one hundred years
on earth you are

a bit bewildered
lost in your red wrinkled skin
and just too tired

to listen to us
who have borrowed a name
for you a hand me down

who are you apart
from laura

the souls of the dead
inhabit the red bean said
the egyptians darkly

and who am I
being here and now blind
to all but laura to say

that some old soul
did not set out
to be

found
among bulrushes
or in the shadow of the bean tree

apart from laura
who are we

my soul is a dark blue stone

Kirovakan, 1971

my soul is a dark blue stone

armenian

and could have happened to anyone walking
on that hard, particular mountain

only would, for the life of me, imagine

and must still, mistakenly
in my worried hand

North Norfolk

This is great grandmother's garden, the flint
ground of her being.   The roodscreen
faces of her saints are diligent, thin.
Her church windows are plain.
God grows out of doors among the tares and stones.
The best of him must go to the malting.
Frost and a bracing wind begot her faith, a plough
share of truth.   The sky is her gaunt grace, her place beneath it
bounded by rivers of reed and alder
and the flint grey sea.

New Year Poem, 1984

I need a holiday in wood or bread
or stone, a hard
mediterranean

light, a big lump of it
and hands that can make it
mourn merrily.

I need a clean wind, hunger
choosing a land
of its own:

not a war
of words or wills or chicken wire
but battles in bone,

in blood. I need those who have died
believing in it, even if
it was stupid.

I need a man and a woman made of light,
between them
not a wooden god, but

one that doubts and ponders
until all that was made
ill is mended.

A house of God my father and my mother made

A house of God my father and my mother made
of my heart.   I am afraid of it.

I can no longer admire it
though it is beautiful and strongly built of stone
brought from the hills.

It is a Portland and a Purbeck heart.

Quickly I strike it with my Moses rod –
that is a rod of iron –
and water rushes over its marble sills

as if the whole sea had, until
this Moses minute,
had to dwell –

as if my heart had been a hospital
civic and capable

and the sea had been ill.

turning from you

you are the wailing wall
where I touch the peculiar sorrow
of my city   watch my shadow
spread   unimpeded   over
these dry stones   there is no one
called god

you are the stony ground
where each seed has unrolled
its bed   and made a shadow
you put out no hands   there is
no holding

you are the blind eye
of the wilderness   there is
no taking in   there is nothing
to do   but swallow down
my shadow   like medicine

I turn from you   to touch
the hem of the horizon   there
is opening of the sky   I know
the bitterness is going from me
now   like rain   the earth drinks in
my shadow

when the rain

for Sarah

when the rain
comes slow   which may be the way
Ruth came through a field of shards   and the world is
no longer a woman gleaning
what little she can from the wind   when the untold
earth sits spinning a cocoon of green
vine like a long yarn
round and round the garden   my old mother
knows   even the stones
are opening

In Southwark Park

for Sarah

There's no sweet night of June about the rose
you borrow
for me: it is golden,
close on red, the middle
evening light a clear grey
after rain.

Nor do you plot your presence. You are
brave enough to be
here: there is no need for me to serve
your fear sweet nothings
on a plate of dust.

If I have bared
the embattled fast stones
of the earth, I believe you are
glad.

The waste of Eden
lies about us, godbones
buried in a concrete yard. We are
the taste of the rain on stone
and thorn –

and all our roses are
stolen.

Reply to your card from the Greek Islands

for Christine

You mention the poppies: it was this time
of the year we waited together
in Crete, for cars to take us over
the dry stone mountains, waited for water,
watched the remote white-painted houses
for signs. It was so hot sometimes
I was afraid.

I'd forgotten the ruins, had almost forgotten you
reading aloud from the guide, your discoveries
turning a footnote into a stone
half-buried in holy ground.

I remember us there, by the road, and always
the poppies blowing along the side
of the wind.

Three Haikus

In Monica's garden

Early morning rain,
the roses a rabble of
light, unreckoning.

Sarah in sleep

Even the island
moon of her loneliness lies
in the sea's navel.

Still life: breakfast

Imperturbable
Stella's half-eaten apple
pie sits in its bowl.

Beginning the avocado

My heart is an avocado
stone in a pot
of earth

but my old truth
my stubborn Elizabeth, my queen
is gone.

She's taken a bath
without telling. The stone
remembers

to root
me in another time
but when

the poem itself splits
open, letting
in

death, the watering
hole of a queen, how am I
to go on?

According to legend, Queen Elizabeth I bathed only once a year.

Spring Evening, Norfolk

for my father

Sun in his red kingly gown
is earlier, gone, which only was
I am or is,
in the vernacular, god, a borrower, lord of

the tree's outline, broken
cradle of buds. What is a garden, wild and orderly
beyond what is, what can be
written down?   I am

beginning, with this April
fire, swift bitter smell of
birch logs, burning – 'blocks'
in a borrowed vernacular – Bede's

history of the English church and people, being
a word for relic, outline, light
left over from the liturgy
of kings.

To be in my words as I

To be in my words as I,
unmetaphorical, may be. To say
the moon is rising, red, behind the woods, which I have seen.

To say not she, not she is my lost one, not that she may be
Lilith, who called herself exiled,
queen of the truth, not she

my solitary one in whom, but moon, which means that
every blade of barley in the bottom field is known by me
to have a shadow of its own.